The first version was me and chaos and horror.

The book happened on its own accord, with my mind somewhere else. I assume it was sleepwalking, while typing in a fog the story of my sister Luda. In that story there were evil husband Borisov and an innocent Luda. I don't see it like this any longer. I don't think she saw it like this either. She was smart, sharp, happy, devoted and she was trouble, somewhat cruel, and asleep. We all are to some degree.

And so one more time, with an apology for the lost words and enchanted English I am to go ahead and try to do it better.

But one thing I can promise - it's not going to be perfect. Not fully edited, not perfect grammar should be expected out of me. I Am Who I Am, - pronounced God something perfect, while perfect should not exist. What is perfect? Something that doesn't change? That is complete? That smells like dead body. I don't know about God being perfect or not, but an answer "I am who I am" is. And for ever will be.

As a child of God, I strongly assume I am, and so everyone else, in my calculation, this is the answer we should all adapt and just go ahead and stop apologizing for who we are.

Shhhhhh! No screaming. I know nothing. I am just blabbering. Like an enchanted, troubled, bruised Soul I walk around this life and have no idea who I am, what I am, where I came from and so on. And those who claim to know - just lying. Not that anything wrong with that. Do what ever that helps you survive this out of any proportion complex life. Just don't hurt anybody intentionally. And try to wake up so that you don't hurt anyone unintentionally either. Love others, yourself. Some day.

For now it's good enough to go ahead and learn step by step this lesson of immense complexity. Hard! F*g hard!

No matter how hard it is to love another, to love yourself is almost impossible. Why? I have an answer to every question, but that doesn't mean even I believe in it. More, I assume it's nothing more but the way to survive in the middle of the ocean, until something saves me.

Sveta A.

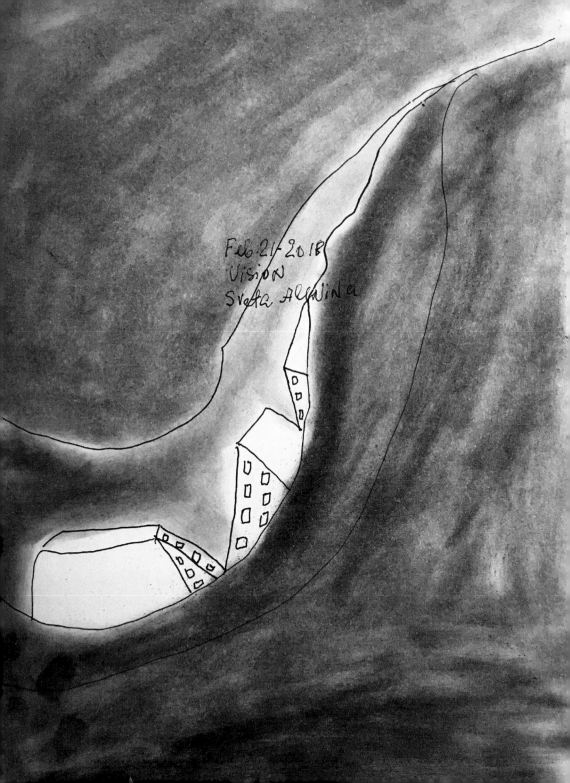

"Scream for Borisov"

Luda, my sister, was in a hospital with a cyst inside her head, which was about to burst out. No stress, not even the lightest, was prescribed by the doctors.

Talk about the right place at the right time: the gift, the wonderful gift.
Borisov, her husband, was next to her.
He brought her papers to sign saying that she is crazy and can't decide her rights on their money. Money earned in fairness to others or not, but in togetherness and lots of danger to the lives of both of them, since the Soviet Union abhors anyone who was trying to make any money by buying and selling products. Anything: be it food brought from the near well-living countries or mascara. The punishment, up to death in Siberia, depending on the size of the bribe and the mood and state of the stomach of the Judge that particular day.
Luda was no more a fearless challenge to him and he got ready. Prepared the ammunition. The tools of murder that are the hardest to be proven in torture or murder: an innocent video on the computer that is easy to delete. Now he had a new lover, aka victim, Yana, who naively believed she was very fortunate to steal her manager's, aka Luda's, husband. Not just fortunate but deserving. That she knew in front of all gods. Who, if not her, deserves what the stupid, sick-on-all-her-head wife-of-the-genius, humble, modest Luda had: the love and devotion of Borisov: The disciplined ex-Captain and proud Mariner. At the time he loved to pronounce Yana's jaw-dropping motto, "Everyone has what he deserves" in front of his grateful audience, in his sexiest voice.

Yes. She didn't believe for a moment that without his black and shiny Mercedes horse and his house (OMG OMG with the gold toilet and the lacey lid) he would be looking so godlike to her. That, I believe, she was unconscious off. In her defense.

The plot lasted years and caused her a lot of sleepless nights.

But, first of all, Borisov wasn't stupid this way.

He knew what Yana, claiming to be in love with him, was after. And he laughed his infamous hyena laugh telling all to broken Luda. And Luda, felt that all this happening to her was a real life horror "I feel like someone put a big spoon in my brain and stirs it".

Luda's personal own God, her Borisov, was telling her about his affair as if nothing was wrong with anything about this story. "I must be crazy. They are right." Believed and didn't believe, my Luda.

Luda was trying to fight Yana, but no one believed Luda. Even our mom hit Luda on the head with the clothes hangers in front of the whole of Luda's store screaming: "Leave poor Yana alone! You are crazy! Crazy!"

When Luda told me about this at the end of her life, I almost died from the realization that what mama did to her that day, was immensely more shocking to Luda than Borisov's part of this story.

he shock was lying like a box full of radiation inside the child-Luda's, body, preserved in the pain not everyone is aware of exists. From her saddest childhood conviction and hope! She is wrong, Luda is wrong, and she will see how mom is just camouflaging her mother's love for Luda out of some silly fear of hurting Luda's upbringing. That fact was the door for Borisov's entry into our lives. As a savior to Luda, and basically a brother to me and a son to our parents.

***

At this point Luda was so full of humiliations from her painful, crazy, against-all-reason family, you would have thought she wouldn't really respond this time either, since she had stopped responding long ago.

Soon after mother's attack she told me, "I don't know why, but I have become so obedient. It petrifies even me..."

***

Our Luda! The Fierce! The warrior who was buried by the mail from all around the world from her adoring friends from the especially gifted athletics-school she went to. She now lived broken by cancer and by the bad luck during a surgery that was trying to remove that cancer, her spine's cancer, literally and psychologically. And not in this order.

From the first sign of her cuckoo behavior everyone considered her bipolar: Crazy. They believed her psychologist, as he was an authority in Luda's life, without ever checking for the organic cause. The cyst in her head was responsible for her sometimes inexplicable behavior. This would have been very easy to explain if only someone tried.

No, it's not all *their* or *our* fault, but Lenin and Vladimir's states of minds as in the foggy, sleepy city of mine on the famous Dnepr river. We were all sleeping and dreaming about living. Even Borisov. Which really doesn't allow anybody to judge any of the players of this drama.

It was fun *and* pain for the whole unconsciously-evil but crazy-in-love-with-each-other family at the same time. We all despaired, and humored each other and circled around Luda's drama after drama. As Jung said: "The family life is circled around the most troubled member." We were tired, and very sick of all this and, of course, endlessly pitying and angered at what seemed to be the constant source of our turbulence: Luda.

At some point, late, way too late, I started to suspect that something was going on here. Something that puzzled me and set me on the path of untangling the entanglement of Eve and Adam. Yes, *that* story. A collective archetype was and is inside each person and within each family and like Bach's Toccata and Fugue in D minor played loudly, "the ceiling fell about all involved heads".

Now she was in Ukraine, Kiev's Third World type of hospital, already operated on once in Zaporojie, where my poor and scared mom was requested to pay $70 for the knife by the doctor who was about to cut Luda's head. He claimed he had no knife. My mom paid of course. She lives in Ukraine and is used to bs! She expects it everywhere she goes. For that she was brought to the most heartbreaking tears by rich Borisov, scolding her for giving away his $70.

"Third World" is *way* above Ukraine. Forgive me for the comparison I used before! Ukraine is a hallucination, a mirage, and that's why not everyone even knows it exists.

The first operation didn't help and we sent her ex-rays to Israel.

Luda's husband, psychopath-under-cover, obsessed with his goal of extinguishing our family, as much as Hitler was with all who were slightly Jewish. Why? Some other time. Paradoxically, he called Israel to find out the results of Luda's brain state and announced to the rest of family that Luda has another cyst: a rare case, fuck our luck, not operational and it's a tragedy, but nothing can be done about it. His face was nothing but a monument to authenticity at that moment.

Everyone started to cry. Each in our own country. Broken families are crying all over the world, now, as the regimes we choose lead us into our bright and promising, *always* promising, futures. I cried and cried, but that was nothing compared to the next stage of the comedy-drama my family life seems to be to me now.

Devil or Angel jerked me to call Israel's hospital:

"This is Luda Borisova's sister."
"Oh yes, yes," answered a very sad voice.
"Can I ask you something...?" I felt very guilty to bother them.
"Her husband said he was told by your hospital that Luda can't be operated on and that it is too late for her, but can I ask you, please: how long does she have?"
".........Shsss???...... we *never* said *that*!!" the nurse answered, in a shocked voice.

Then, silence.

"WE NEVER SAID THAT" screamed, right from the sky, the enlarged building of Israel's hospital. At least that was the vision I had of the hospital building, full of people looking through the windows at me, with horror screaming for ever, and very loud. So loud I couldn't understand for some time what they were saying.

Then I heard: "We said...what we said...is that she must be brought to us and operated on immediately or her cyst might break and kill her at any moment."

"Also," said the nurses voice, that already replaced the screaming hospital, "we said that there is a risk that she might die in the airplane. She might even die on the operating table. Why did you wait so long?"

I said, "We were busy laughing at her. We were busy gossiping about her." Isn't it funny, really? For all the generations back and back it's probably the funniest show.

But she ignored such a "joke" and added, "We also estimate her coffin delivery (God forbid) to be US$30,000 and the operation another US $30,000."

Next I found myself standing beside my daughter Julie, who was asking Borisov on the phone "Uncle Yuriy, how could you do this?"

He said: "I have no money."

Yes, just like that. Like the whole world should understand this obstacle without any further explanation.

"But," asked Julie, who he really respected and maybe even loved, "Uncle Yura...you showed us many albums full of real golden, historic, priceless dollars that you won at those auctions you went to for years for $30, while their real price was $250,000 each...?"

Too late realizing his weakness, Borisov shooshed, "None of your business!"

"But uncle Yura...it was also her money...also hers..." My little Julie met the Devil face to face for the first time, minutes before I did.

Then we laid on the floor and the airplane fell on us from the sky, and we didn't move a second for the next three years.

***

Back to when Luda was in the hospital in Kiev, Ukraine: I am in Boston and she surprises me by telling me...

When Borisov went out she called me and said: "Sveta, can you believe this? He makes me look at him having sex with his lover, Yana. He laughs, cowardly."

I will omit my reaction, as this kind of crap really makes one feel like one is in a dream, especially when said crap is pronounced calmly and not with humour!

"He wants me to sign the papers. In short, no money for me."

Less than anything I was concerned about her *having* or *not* having money. I begged him (Fuck! I just remembered!) I begged: "Let her go... let her die next to me. Keep all your money. I will leave you alone. I will not try and spoil your life. I will forget you exist." He refused calmly, thoroughly enjoying executing me. Me, his biggest enemy and obsession. And I could not figure out why. Not yet. At the time it started I was living far away, full of respect and love for him as my brother-in-law.

I have no idea what kind of an invalid he made out of Luda, at this point, as we were very carefully separated from each other by Borisov for many years. He felt our connection since our childhood when we all *grew up together* in the buildings of the families of the mariners. Even though she was pretty much cruel to me, I'm sure it was out of the pain of not being loved by mama. Did she have a nightmare about mama being a petrifying unloving witch, who ate her *real* mama? I don't know. But we will pay for it. All the family and each of us will pay *dearly*, for all our lives. At the same time she was my biggest defender and her pain would transfer into running-energy to catch and punish the boys who made me cry. Anyone who had the nerve to forget that I was Luda's sister, even if they only hurt me accidentally, paid dearly for my tears.

We played. We were kids. She was full of pain and she ran like a wild panther. Which was *somehow* noticed by the Soviet Union and she was "chosen" as a sacrifice (at least that's how she felt every minute for 8 years afterwards). She was chosen as an especially gifted athlete and all that was sporty and off she went away from mama to that prestigious school.

We were standing by the bath tub. I even remember the type of most-depressing light that was in the air. Mixed with black. I remember, too, as any kid sees what adults don't, there were black spots in the air, formed out of her sadness, waves of black, mixed into each other forming the appropriate backdrop to what we felt.

"Why don't you let me hug you?" I asked in my mind, and her silent answer fell on me like a bomb and went straight into my unconscious. She simply communicated to me a fact: "Because Kassya," (she called me Kassya then – that's a long separate story) "this woe is not a temporary woe. It is ours forever."

And she went away, not looking back even once. And Fuck, I just realized, not walked to the bus by anyone.

Skinny, eight-year-old sadness manifested under her arm holding the box of some game. For some reason I don't know why this seemed very out of place to five year old Kassya. What a weird, freakishly wired memory I have.

**** Nothing is in any particular order in this story. Working on this book is not at all good for me and so I let it be as it pours.***

Her anger and tears and life's unfairness collided and formed the potential for something as powerful as an atomic bomb.

"To be or not to be?" In pain, my noble and loving father tried to decide. But the whining, as always mother's voice, and who could blame him? Not many will get it, but she was *Mother Nature* herself. No one couldn't not see that she was the Great and Evil, in one package.

I was left in this part of the story by Luda for eight years, and lived a good life. Masha soon was born. I was basically left alone, with my zombie-like life with flowers in a yard. My favorites wild and not educated.

It was a good childhood. Whenever dad could, I was taken to his freight ship. We got along perfectly then.

But back to the land of another dimension. I seriously don't want to go in there as I know for sure I slept in a fog until recently, collecting facts that were so awful that they would drop into the unconsciousness and re-surface or start to slowly show above the dark, muddy waters of my strange memory on this day of Luda's call to me from Ukraine's hospital.

***

It didn't even hit me because they were always the most strange couple to me. An Enigma I didn't care that much to solve. Luda was getting farther and farther from me, affected, as she was, by the constantly turned-on radio right inside her ear called, "The Voice of Borisov". He sings, tear in his eyes, almost always, for some reason, as if laughing king of tears: Nobody loves you. Not Sveta, not Masha... How envious I am of his dedication to exterminate my family and for what reason I might never figure out why. It could be my scream, as much as anything else, like his nightmare that he took for reality.

Surprised that she all-of-a-sudden decided to confide in me, I said: "Why don't you kick him out of there?".

"Haha! Why? He is trying to kill me and I will do the same to him."

I don't judge, I am bleeding now. My role is to describe and your role is to do whatever you want with it. I don't care. I want to go back home with or without a trophy. Sick of it all, hardly alive, I must write this book, which makes me want to throw up. But the creative spirit, as wittily noted by Carl Jung, doesn't care about the writer or artist's health and well being, it only cares about the end result: goodness for everyone.

If not for this, true or not, I believe I would run amok at this very point.

Haha is all there is left to say. Because you may think: Sveta, *chill*. It can't get any worse. But, here it comes, a lot a lot a lot worse, and so on.

Anyway...he came back, I screamed at him and he ran away, as the coward he really was. Is. Will be. I hope not. I hope everything goes through the Alchemical Process that Life is and at the end we will dance and laugh together.

And Borisov, as when we were allright with each other, will laugh and say: "Svetka, Svetka! Remember?"

And I will stare at him with my frozen face, waiting for the story finally.

And he will say: "Remember you thought I was evil? Remember you yelled at me for the first time and I ran away?"

And we will become two balloons and laugh and float bouncing against each other.

Mama! Luda! Borisov! Let's live in peace! How hard is it?

And God will say: "Kids, we did good, we did an excellent job, the most hard job ever! We become Love!"

This fairy tale, true or not-true-tale, is the the only reason I am breathing right now and writing this book here in the Colonial house I am currently in, doing my job, hating and loving it, being proud as a soldier, and doubting it is needed, all at the same time.***

***

You know? I don't want to go into details any longer.
My first version did a little.
With grammar that some called "Enchanted English" it was published and hated by some but loved by others. Duplicity is the core and the source of anything alive. The book itself breathed its first breath and cried to the world: "The scream for Borisov!" in the smallest details spooking Borisov as much or much more than the scream of little five year old Sveta every time she saw little Borisov.

The scream, no one could figure, that lasted until she was red and almost fainting. The scream no one could explain. The scream she forgot all about until reminded by Borisov when adults. The scream that would visit Borisov again and again in his nightmares for all his life.

Why? Because when he is finally finished with Luda, Sveta starts writing incessantly: the poems with words describing her dreams and publishing them with all their typos:
I SAW OUR MURDERED LUDA ...
IN HER GENTLY LACED COFFIN...
IN HER TINY SNEAKERS
IN MY DREAM...last night.....
****

Fine.

Can I please forever forget all this, God? Now that it's on paper. Please?

Do you even hear me?

Do you even know my name? It's Crazy Sveta, remember?

Do you even exist? Or are you mad at me? Or are you also mad, as I am?

****

"I BELIEVE IN NOTHINNESS" stated my dad's tattoo. My only inheritance. The tattoo that marked yet another tragedy of betrayal of the dancing-naked-on-the-table beloved first wife, with whom he had a very good son, Fedia. And this son of his was *also* a captain, and was *also* betrayed by his wife, who he ran away from.

The next we heard of him or about him:

The red phone on the fridge. I pick up. "Dad, it's for you."

Dad comes toward me and I make fun of his morbid face – a look I'd never ever noted on him before. He kindly chuckles at me and picks up the phone.

Who is it? Your lover?

I see his back. He is going into his room and closes the door behind him.

"What's with him?" I ask mom, after she talks to dad.

"Fedia was swallowed by the wave from his yacht into the too-cold water and raging waves and the whole city of mariners is in shock."

He was loved. He was adored for his fierceness and what not... He left behind my dad and his forever-regretting-loosing-my-father-as-her-husband mom. Fedia adored his mother and she showed me his letters as if they were written to the most beautiful creature on earth or in heaven. Even at her age she had a polished, beautiful face with which she looked pained and angry. She looked just like Fedia. Woe crook-ed her face and she turned around and walked away.

believe in nothing but pain. Mine and everything alive.

Don't make me even start on this one.

Beause I didn't even begin to tell this story but as I see no end it doesn't matter where it stops.....

I write this book against the constant feeling of bile and poison it makes me feel, even though I am convinced as it gets out it will become an eye opener for many. Hopefully preventing, *Please* for the sake of all the Invisible Powers, preventing at least as many as one lost and confused, entangled family of loving, really loving-each-other trees. Torn from each other and knowing the pain, will grow with its help into the psychic advance, which Life is. Life is pain. Yes. In the ass. Hahahaha.............. or not hahahahahaha.

sveta alenina. 2020. the end.

Sveta A.

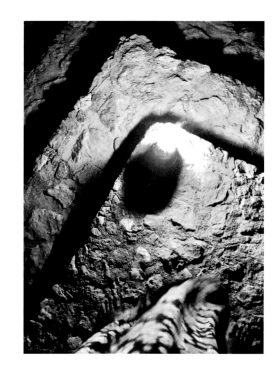

Lightning Source UK Ltd.
Milton Keynes UK
UKRC011427030820
367276UK00022B/129